EYEWITNESS TO
THE RUSSIAN REVOLUTION

BY LYDIA BJORNLUND

Published by The Child's World®
1980 Lookout Drive • Mankato, MN 56003-1705
800-599-READ • www.childsworld.com

Photographs ©: AP Images, cover, 1, 19, 22; Everett Historical/Shutterstock Images, 5, 8, 14, 28; George Shuklin, 6; Album/Kurwenal/Prisma/Newscom, 10; Fine Art Images Heritage Images/Newscom, 12; akg-images/Newscom, 15, 26; Ann Ronan Picture Library Heritage Images/Newscom, 16; Heritage Image Partnership Ltd/Alamy, 18; dpa picture alliance/Alamy, 21; Library of Congress, 25

ISBN 9781503816060

LCCN 2016945605

Printed in the United States of America
PA02317

ABOUT THE AUTHOR

Lydia Bjornlund is a full-time freelance writer and author of more than two dozen children's books. She has a master's degree in education from Harvard University and a bachelor's degree in American studies from Williams College. She lives in northern Virginia with her husband, Gerry Hoetmer, and their two children, Jake and Sophia.

TABLE OF CONTENTS

FAST FACTS

What was the Russian Revolution?

- The Russian Revolution started in 1917. Russian workers started to protest against the government.

- The workers were against Russia's involvement in World War I (1914–1918). Many Russians were dying in the war. The war was also causing food and supply shortages throughout Russia.

Who was Nicholas II?

- **Czar** Nicholas II was the ruler of Russia. He was a member of the Romanov family. The Romanovs had ruled Russia since 1613.

- The protesters forced Nicholas II to give up the throne in March 1917.

Who was Vladimir Lenin?

- Vladimir Lenin was the leader of the Bolsheviks. The Bolsheviks were a group that took over Russia's government in the fall of 1917.

- Lenin and the Bolsheviks were communists. Communism is a system in which all property is owned by the government.

What were the results of the Russian Revolution?

- New leaders took over the Russian government. They withdrew Russia from World War I on March 3, 1918, with the Treaty of Brest-Litovsk.

- The revolution ended with the creation of the Union of Socialist Soviet Republics (USSR) in 1922.

Chapter 1

FROM RIOT TO REVOLT

March 8, 1917, was a sunny day in the Russian capital of Petrograd. Women all around the city were glad to get outside. It had been a cold winter. The women left their homes to celebrate International Women's Day. International Women's Day is a yearly celebration. But this year, the women did not believe they had much to celebrate. It was the third year of Russia's involvement in World War I.

◄ **Women take to the streets on International Women's Day to protest Russia's involvement in World War I.**

Many women had lost sons, husbands, brothers, and friends during the war.

The war had made things difficult in other ways. Fewer trains carrying food and goods rolled into Petrograd. Women spent hours waiting in long lines in the freezing cold to purchase flour, bread, and other supplies. When the women were not in line, they worked long hours in factories alongside men who were too young, too old, or not strong enough to fight in the war.

The women marched in the streets. They carried signs and began to chant for peace and for bread. A growing number of Russians blamed the czar, Nicholas II, for their problems. They blamed him for leading Russia to war in Europe and for the food shortages the war caused.

For the next several days, the crowd grew. Thousands of male workers joined the women. These men were on strike demanding better working conditions. Soon approximately 100,000 people had joined the bread riots. Police officers asked the protesters to return to their homes. But the protesters ignored the requests. Angry mobs destroyed property and police stations. Someone in the mob said they intended to "destroy all Government offices [and] burn, smash, kill all police."[1]

▲ **Nicholas II had taken command of the Russian army in late 1915.**

Mikhail Rodzianko, a Russian politician, sent a message to Nicholas II. "Situation serious. There is **anarchy** in the capital," the message said.[2]

Nicholas II was away with troops in western Russia when the message arrived. At first he did not take the warning seriously.

He called the message "nonsense to which I will not even reply."[3] A couple days later, the czar decided he needed to do something. He ordered the military to shoot any protester who would not back down.

The order backfired. The soldiers did not want to fire upon their fellow citizens. The soldiers understood the protesters' situation. And so, one by one, soldiers switched sides. They joined the protests against the czar.

"Our fathers, mothers, sisters, brothers, and brides are begging for bread. Are we going to kill them?"

—Russian soldier, on being asked to attack the protesters[4]

Within days, those loyal to Nicholas II were outnumbered. On March 15, Nicholas II agreed to give up his position as czar. It had been one week since the women took to the streets to ask for bread. Nicholas II asked his brother Mikhail to take over the job. Mikhail turned down the offer. For the first time in 300 years, Russia had no czar.

Chapter 2

THE PROVISIONAL GOVERNMENT

Alexander Kerensky smiled with satisfaction. He had hoped this day would come. In 1912 he had been elected to the Duma. The Duma was a government body Nicholas II had started in 1905. It was supposed to give Russians a voice in their government. But the Duma had little power.

◄ **Demonstrators gather outside of Tauride Palace in March 1917.**

Nicholas II **disbanded** it any time its members disagreed with his actions. Kerensky believed it was the czar, not the Duma, who needed to go. So when the czar gave up the throne, Kerensky believed it was Russia's chance to create a better government.

Kerensky met with other members of the Duma at Tauride Palace in Petrograd. They were going to choose leaders for a **provisional** government. Thousands of people waited outside to hear the results. When the leaders were announced, there was uproar. The people were shocked at what they heard. The new government included no members of the working class. Instead, it was made up of wealthy Russians. Prince George Lvov was announced as the new leader. In response, one soldier cried out, "You mean all we did was exchange a czar for a prince?"[5]

The people applauded when they heard Kerensky was to be the new minister of justice. Kerensky was not a member of the working class. But as a lawyer he had earned the trust of the poor by fighting on their behalf.

Kerensky took advantage of his power. He moved the provisional government to the Winter Palace. The palace was usually the home of the czar. Kerensky held meetings in the czar's dining room. He had photos of himself taken at the czar's desk.

As minister of justice, Kerensky freed people who had been jailed or **exiled** for speaking out against the government. Russians could again freely write and speak. Kerensky said that Russia was the freest country in the world.

But the government did little to help those who were suffering from the effects of the war. Also, the government had little power to apply its laws. So the people followed only the laws they liked. People gathered together in towns throughout Russia. They

"One can say flatly that the Provisional Government exists only so long as it is permitted by the [Petrograd] Soviet."

—*Alexander Guchkov, minister of war of the provisional government*[6]

formed their own governments, called **soviets**. These groups soon became more powerful than the provisional government.

Meanwhile, in Petrograd, Kerensky and the new leaders kept Russia in World War I. In the summer of 1917, they ordered Russian troops to move against German and Austrian forces. But the Russian military was faring poorly in battle. Many Russian soldiers thought their country should pull out of the war.

◀ **Alexander Kerensky sits in the czar's desk of the Winter Palace.**

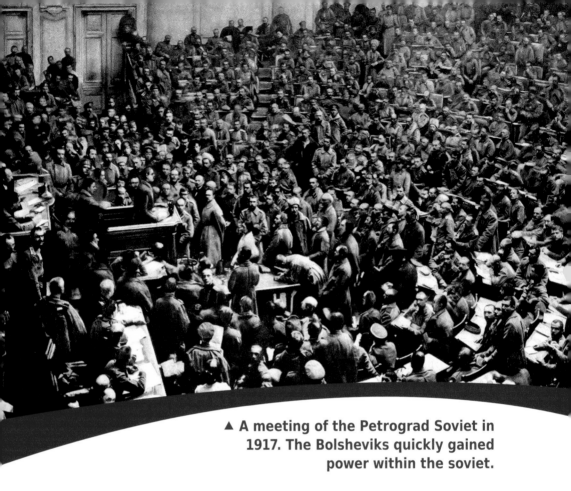

▲ **A meeting of the Petrograd Soviet in 1917. The Bolsheviks quickly gained power within the soviet.**

Russian soldiers refused to leave their trenches to fight. Thousands boarded trains and headed home.

The Russian people were angry with the provisional government. On July 17, hundreds of thousands of people flocked into the streets of Petrograd. They chanted, "All power to the soviets!"[7] Violence broke out. By the end of the day, hundreds of protesters' bodies lay scattered on the streets. Lvov gave up his position because of the riots. Kerensky became the new leader.

Kerensky knew his government was in danger. Many groups demanded fast change. The most powerful group was the Bolshevik Party. Bolsheviks believed the revolution would not be finished until all people shared power.

▲ **Pro-soviet protesters march in the streets of Petrograd before being attacked by government troops on July 17, 1917.**

Chapter 3

THE BOLSHEVIKS TAKE POWER

Vladimir Lenin read the news of the bread riots from Switzerland. Lenin was the leader of the Bolsheviks. He had been forced to leave Russia 12 years earlier because of his **revolutionary** ideas.

In April 1917, Lenin secretly returned to Petrograd. He got in touch with a number of officials in the Russian government. Among them was Leon Trotsky. Trotsky was the chairman of the Petrograd Soviet.

With Trotsky's support, the Petrograd Soviet voted to support Lenin's Bolshevik Party. The Bolsheviks began recruiting people to help them take over the government by force. They called their soldiers the Red Guard.

On the night of November 6, the Red Guard spread throughout Petrograd. They wore ill-fitting uniforms and held rifles with **bayonets**. They took up positions at telegraph offices, power plants, and railroad stations. The Red Guard faced little resistance from government soldiers. Overnight, they controlled much of the city.

On November 7, food supplies to the Winter Palace were cut off. Guards abandoned their posts. A few young recruits and female soldiers remained to defend the palace. Kerensky had heard talk that an attack might take place. He borrowed a car and left Petrograd to recruit soldiers to protect the government.

That evening, a cannon shot rang out from a ship in Petrograd's harbor. It was the signal the Red Guard was waiting for. Thousands of members of the Red Guard stormed the Winter Palace. Scattered gunfire rang out through the palace. But the Bolsheviks encountered little resistance. They arrested the leaders of the provisional government.

From outside the city, Kerensky spoke to reporters. He said he would hold the Bolsheviks accountable for their actions. Kerensky gathered soldiers to help him take Petrograd. But within days, they were defeated. The Bolsheviks took over the government.

▲ **Bolsheviks storm the Winter Palace on November 7, 1917.**

▲ **Bolshevik leaders inspect a row of Cheka, or secret police, in 1921.**

Lenin and the Bolsheviks were communists. They believed in sharing wealth equally. They took land from churches and the rich and gave it to peasant families to farm. The party got rid of titles and ranks to show that all Russians were equal. The Bolshevik government also took over factories and mines.

Lenin knew there were many people who did not agree with his government. He worried someone would rise up against him. Lenin created a group of secret police called the Cheka.

> "We have won Russia from the rich for the poor, from the exploiters for the working people."
>
> —*Vladimir Lenin, April 1918*[8]

In the following months and years, the Cheka would carry out Lenin's severe orders. The Cheka used intimidation and violence against anyone who spoke out against the Bolshevik government.

From the beginning, Lenin and the Bolsheviks had gained popularity by promising to take Russia out of World War I. On December 15, 1917, Russia and the Central Powers agreed to stop fighting each other. Trotsky traveled to Brest-Litovsk, in present-day Belarus, to discuss terms for peace. The meeting ended when Trotsky stormed out. He said Germany's terms were unacceptable.

Fighting started again in February. Russian troops once again fared poorly. Disheartened, Lenin signed the Treaty of Brest-Litovsk on March 3, 1918. In exchange for peace, Russia gave Germany 1 million square miles (1.6 million sq km) of land. This land was home to approximately 55 million people. Russia also lost almost one-third of its farm production, one-quarter of its industry, and three-quarters of its coal and iron supply.

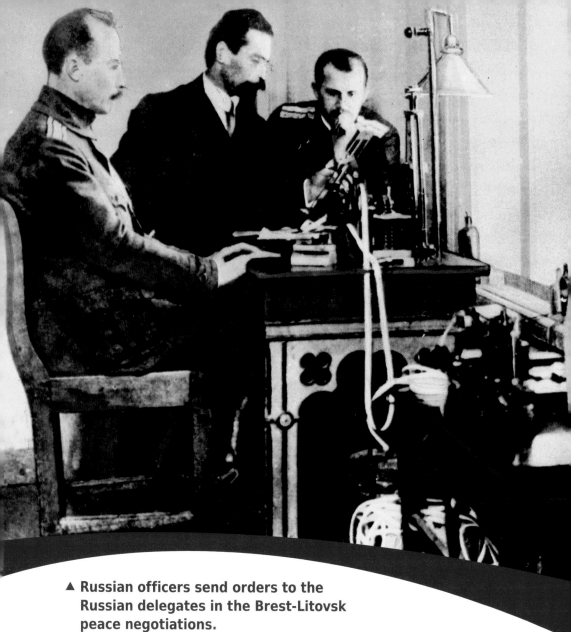

▲ Russian officers send orders to the
Russian delegates in the Brest-Litovsk
peace negotiations.

Lenin was upset about the heavy losses. However, he believed

he had made the right choice. He hoped to spread communism

to countries other than Russia. To do this, he believed there

needed to be peace.

Chapter 4

WAR AND CHAOS

In the early hours of July 17, 1918, a Bolshevik doctor woke Nicholas II and his wife, Alexandra, and told them to get dressed. The doctor also woke the couple's son and four daughters. The doctor told the family they were being moved for their own safety.

Anti-Bolshevik forces were approaching the city of Yekaterinburg, where the family was being held.

◀ **The Bolsheviks confined the Romanovs to a guarded house in Yekaterinburg in 1918.**

The Romanovs hoped they would be freed from the Bolsheviks at last.

Nicholas II and his family had been living under guard since he had given up the throne more than a year earlier. Yekaterinburg was the third place the family had lived. The Romanovs had first been kept at their palace in Petrograd. But government leaders feared pro-czarist groups would free the family and try to put Nicholas II back in power. They moved the family to an estate in Siberia, a far-off part of Russia.

While in Siberia, Nicholas II had spent his days tending to the grounds of the estate or taking long walks. The family had spent their evenings reading together and playing cards. The guards had watched the family closely, but they had allowed the Romanovs much freedom. There was no way the Romanovs could have left the area on foot.

Then Nicholas heard the Bolsheviks had taken power. He had followed the events with interest. He hoped the new government would allow him and his family to leave the country. Members of the provisional government had planned to allow the Romanovs to leave. But the Bolsheviks had no such plans.

After the Bolsheviks took power, new guards had arrived to watch the family. Other big changes had occurred, too. The cupboards had run out of butter and coffee. These items were limited, and the Bolsheviks believed in equality. This meant the family ate the same **rations** as soldiers. It also meant there were no servants in the house. The Bolshevik guards had kept the family under close supervision. They had stopped Nicholas II from walking the grounds.

The Romanovs had spent eight months in Siberia. Then the Bolsheviks became worried. They thought Nicholas II's supporters were on their way to save him. That was how Nicholas II and his family had ended up in the small two-story house in Yekaterinburg, a town in central Russia. After the Romanovs arrived, guards had painted over the windows. The Romanovs were prohibited from opening them. The children all shared a bedroom on the upper floor. Their parents slept in a nearby bedroom.

Nicholas II and his family had made the best of their new situation. After eating a simple breakfast of black bread and tea, they spent most of their time sitting in the small garden or playing cards. All the while, they held out hope the government would allow them to leave the country.

▲ **The Bolsheviks ordered that the Romanovs be killed in order to prevent a potential uprising.**

When they were awakened on July 17, the Romanovs quietly followed their guards to the basement of the home. The guards brought chairs for Nicholas, Alexandra, and their son, who was sick. When the family was in place, the guards carried out their orders. The entire family was shot and killed.

Chapter 5

A NEW ORDER

The execution of the Romanovs was only part of the Bolsheviks' plan to stay in power. From the beginning, there was opposition to the new government. Some Russians wanted to put the czar back in place. Others called for elections to choose their leaders. Even people who had supported the Bolsheviks became upset. Throughout Russia, starvation was still a big problem.

Within months of taking power, the Bolsheviks were faced with strong resistance. A **civil war** began. People no longer trusted the Bolsheviks. Members of the government started calling themselves communists instead. The people who fought the communists' Red Army were called the Whites.

The war was long and bloody. Trotsky became the leader of the Red Army. He was a stern leader. He executed officers found guilty of cowardice. Those who did well in battle were quickly promoted. The Bolsheviks closed down newspapers that printed bad things about them. The party also banned other political parties and arrested anyone who challenged them.

In an interview, Felix Dzerzhinsky, the head of the Cheka, defended the government's actions. "Terror is an absolute necessity during times of revolution," he said. "Our aim is to fight against the enemies of the soviet government."[9]

The White Army also used violent methods. They stole crops and livestock to feed their soldiers. Anyone who objected faced terrible consequences. The White Army also burned entire towns they believed supported the Bolsheviks.

For almost three years, the two sides battled for control of the country. In 1920 the Red Army defeated the White Army.

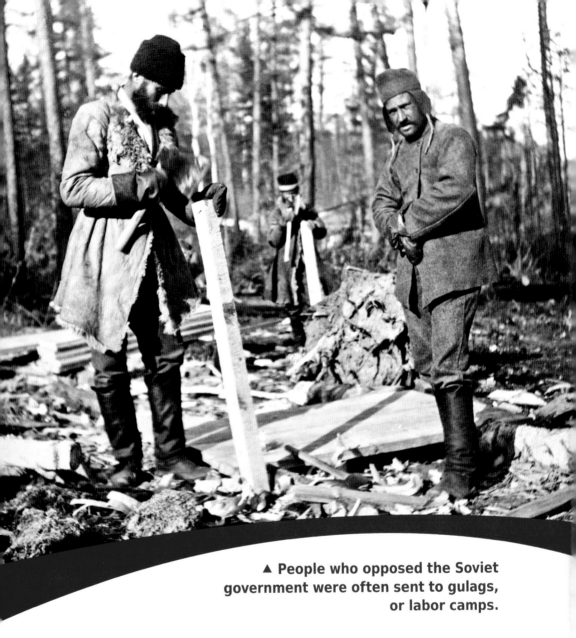

▲ People who opposed the Soviet government were often sent to gulags, or labor camps.

After the war, the country was badly damaged. Fields lay burned. Bridges, railroads, and factories were destroyed. More than 8 million Russians had lost their lives to starvation, illness, and **exposure**.

The government started to rebuild. It built roads and schools. It set up health services and encouraged the arts and sciences. Lenin, Trotsky, and other Russian leaders believed that communism was the best system for the people. In 1922 they established the United Soviet Socialist Republics (USSR).

People in the USSR had a hard time achieving the dream Lenin had offered. The system of communism lasted for approximately 70 years. In the early 1990s the people once again demanded change. For the first time, Russia's leaders allowed people to share ideas and speak out against the government. Communism fell, and a time of more open and democratic government began.

THINK ABOUT IT

- Nicholas II was away at the front lines when the bread riots broke out in Petrograd. At first he did not take the riots seriously. Do you think he could have done anything differently to stop the riots and the revolution? Why or why not?
- How did World War I contribute to the Russian Revolution?
- If you were Lenin, would you have signed the Treaty of Brest-Litovsk? Why or why not?

GLOSSARY

anarchy (AN-er-kee): Anarchy is a situation of disorder and lack of authority. Anarchy broke out in Petrograd in 1917.

bayonets (BAY-uh-nets): Bayonets are blades that attach to the ends of rifles. The Bolsheviks attached their bayonets before attacking.

civil war (SIV-ull WAR): A civil war is a fight between different groups within the same country. The Red Army won the Russian Civil War.

czar (ZAHR): The czar was the emperor of Russia. Nicholas II became czar after his father, Alexander III, died.

disbanded (dis-BAND-ed): Something is disbanded when it is broken up or stops functioning. Nicholas II often disbanded the Duma.

exiled (EG-ziled): To be exiled is to be sent away without being able to return. Vladimir Lenin was exiled for political reasons.

exposure (ik-SPOH-zhur): Exposure is the harmful effect of severe weather on the body. Many Russians died from exposure before the civil war ended in 1920.

provisional (pruh-VIZH-uh-null): Something that is provisional is temporary or not final. Alexander Kerensky led the provisional government for a short time.

rations (RASH-uhns): Rations are limited amounts of food and supplies. Soldiers at war receive daily rations.

revolutionary (rev-uh-LOO-shuhn-ner-ee): Something is revolutionary if it involves sudden, far-reaching change. The Bolsheviks had revolutionary ideas.

soviets (SOH-vee-ets): Soviets were local government bodies. The soviets gained more power than the provisional government.

SOURCE NOTES

1. Pitirim Aleksandrovich Sorokin. *Leaves from a Russian Diary*. Boston, MA: Beacon Press. Print. 3.

2. "Russian Revolution Quotations." *Alpha History*. Alpha History, 2016. Web. 2 Aug 2016.

3. Ibid.

4. John D. Loscher. *The Bolsheviks*. Bloomington, IN: AuthorHouse, 2009. Print. 335.

5. Orlando Figes. *Revolutionary Russia, 1891–1991*. New York: Metropolitan, 2014. Print. 77.

6. Sheila Fitzpatrick. *The Russian Revolution*. New York: Oxford UP, 2008. Print. 47.

7. Richard G. Hovannisian. *Armenia on the Road to Independence, 1918*. Berkeley, CA: University of California Press. Print. 83.

8. Ronald Clark. *Lenin: The Man Behind the Mask*. London, UK: Bloomsbury, 2011. Print. 403.

9. Mikkel Thorup. *An Intellectual History of Terror*. New York: Routledge, 2010. Print. 108.

TO LEARN MORE

Books

Fleming, Candace. *The Family Romanov.* New York: Schwartz & Wade, 2014.

Rasmussen, R. Kent. *World War I for Kids.* Chicago, IL: Chicago Review Press, 2014.

Whiting, Jim. *The Russian Revolution, 1917.* Hockessin, DE: Mitchell Lane, 2008.

Web Sites

Visit our Web site for links about the Russian Revolution:

childsworld.com/links

Note to Parents, Teachers, and Librarians: We routinely verify our Web links to make sure they are safe and active sites. So encourage your readers to check them out!

INDEX